For Today
and
Tomorrow

For Today and Tomorrow

Carroll Blair

Aveon Publishing Company

ISBN: 978-1-936430-27-7

Library of Congress Control Number
2011904311

Aveon Publishing Co.
P.O. Box 380739
Cambridge, MA 02238-0739 USA

Also by Carroll Blair

Grains of Thought
Facing the Circle
Reel to Real
Shifting Tides
Reaches
Out of Silence
Quarter Notes
By Rays of Light
Into the Inner Life
Gnosis of the Heart
Soul Reflections
Beneath and Beyond the Surface
Of Courage and Commitment
In Meditation
Sightings Along the Journey
Through Desert's Fire
Offerings to Pilgrims
Human Natures
(Of Animal and Spiritual)
Atoms from the Suns of Solitude
Colors of Devotion
Voicings
Through the Shadows
As the World Winds Flow

For Today and Tomorrow

What is forever has always been with you.

Life awaits all to speak its essence through the voice of the eternal.

For Today and Tomorrow

*T*he days of your life are not without end, but may be filled with the never-ending.

*O*nly in the temporal is today and tomorrow able to disappoint.

For Today and Tomorrow

$\mathcal{T}$he day is missed for one who has not gleaned from it the timeless of its presence.

$\mathcal{M}$ore than a simple opening of one's eyes is an awakening to the dawn.

For Today and Tomorrow

*L*ife is always fresh and alive teeming with divine energy and light, the enlightened spirit rejoicing in its majesty, living through it, by it, for it.

*W*orthy of reverence at every moment is Life, and it is they who revere it who are most inspired.

For Today and Tomorrow

*T*ime is a transport from birth to death, but in the interim one may step away from it [spiritually] and join with eternity.

*T*o live substantively is to fill one's days with thought and activity that could well be thought and done in any tomorrow, their substance not passing with the day.

For Today and Tomorrow

*O*nly that part of a life truly *lives*
which is joined to the eternal.

*I*n the spiritual realm flowerings
are ever bourgeoning with beauty
into light.

For Today and Tomorrow

*F*ood taken into the body nourishes for a
day; nourishment for the spirit is for now
and all the days that follow.

*L*ife holds infinite insights that have yet
to be revealed, each day opening itself in
invitation to make their discovery.

For Today and Tomorrow

*Y*our life is a transitory gift holding within it (within you) what is eternal, to be ignored or embraced.

*I*s it wise to stake anything on the comings and goings of the fleeting?

For Today and Tomorrow

What value has that which can be replaced?

All that is fleeting dwarfs in the presence of the eternal.

For Today and Tomorrow

*O*ne's spirit rises by shedding more and more of the temporal from one's life.

*N*othing of the temporal is strongly centered, swept this way and that like leaves on grass. Only the life lived through the eternal cannot be turned by outward event or circumstance.

For Today and Tomorrow

*T*o live through the eternal is not to live each day the same, but to live by its light, which remains the same.

*T*he light never stops revealing, never stops drawing and inspiring to greater awareness.

For Today and Tomorrow

*T*he eye is not properly focused, the mind not properly set that doesn't go beyond the particular on to the universal.

*W*hat has substance today will have it tomorrow, and for all tomorrows.

For Today and Tomorrow

$\mathcal{T}$o live deeply and fully one must do away with fear of the inevitable annihilation of the physical, living with and for what time cannot sweep away.

$\mathcal{W}$hat does it matter where one is in the material universe when one's focus is on the sublime?

For Today and Tomorrow

No one would trade pearls for dust, but how often have pearls of the spirit been given up for dust of the fleeting.

There is nothing less than profound in the realm of the spiritual; there is nothing close to profound in the realm of the temporal.

For Today and Tomorrow

*I*t is in life's highest planes where hints to the scale of metaphysical power can be sensed.

*W*hat is worth embracing whose essence fades with the day?

For Today and Tomorrow

*T*here are lasting gifts in every day
of life to be appreciated and accepted or
to pass them by in pursuit of the trivial.

*I*s your life not worth the best of Life,
which has nothing to do with the temporal?

For Today and Tomorrow

"*Y*es" and "no" are not only words that are spoken, but also lived.

*T*he light of a day signifies hope and reminds one that there is a choice to let more light of the eternal into one's life.

For Today and Tomorrow

*T*here is no moment that is not a right moment for endeavor toward spiritual growth.

*T*he days pass, but not the results of what is done for the maturing of qualities of a higher nature.

For Today and Tomorrow

What is strived for in the spiritual will always be received, providing the effort is complete.

A step is taken, but what is the point if not followed by another . . .

For Today and Tomorrow

$\mathcal{N}$ot every step of the spiritual journey is surrounded by beauty, but its aim is ever toward the beautiful.

$\mathcal{E}$ach day brings another opportunity to fulfill the promise of a life, and celebrate the gift and miracle that is Life.

For Today and Tomorrow

*T*he spirit able to rest well at the close of the day is the one that rose with purpose at its beginning.

*T*o have no attachments to the temporal is to align one's energies with the indestructible.

For Today and Tomorrow

*O*nly what is inspired by the eternal can move the spirit to its best.

*T*he one true power is that of the spiritual . . . of the eternal.

For Today and Tomorrow

To not work for spiritual growth is to fall prey to the wiles of the fleeting.

To be ever vigilant of the darkness that is taken for light in the affairs of everyday life is to be spiritually aware.

For Today and Tomorrow

A folly dies and in its place a wisdom is born.

A human being is the only entity on earth, perhaps in the universe that knows abstractly yet clearly that there will be a tomorrow . . . is this not an awesome responsibility to tomorrow?

For Today and Tomorrow

*H*ow often throughout humankind
are the needs of tomorrow jeopardized
for frivolous wants of today.

*E*very day is judgment day.

For Today and Tomorrow

*L*ife is more, *much more* than the
surface-based stimuli of day-to-day living.

*T*hey see only the kindergarten of life
who see only the temporal.

For Today and Tomorrow

The day invites all to *life*, and how much it is betrayed by pursuit of the dying.

There is higher life, deeper life waiting to be lived.

For Today and Tomorrow

*T*he sun shines above, but what is its light to the one who hasn't reached the sun lighting within?

*W*hen growth of a spiritual nature is observed in a human being it is more beautiful than a spring flower blossoming into being.

For Today and Tomorrow

What better companions can accompany one throughout the day than love, truth, courage, generosity, and discipline?

The primary goal of all higher teaching is to awaken the contribution within.

For Today and Tomorrow

*I*f man should take one lesson from life it's that it holds nothing back, giving all it has to give.

*W*orking the spiritual will sometimes get the better of you, but it will also draw the best from you.

For Today and Tomorrow

*B*eing better tomorrow than one is today will not always be achieved, but what excuse is there for not trying to be?

*A*ll that you are is never all that you can be.

For Today and Tomorrow

Should not the least to do in the
improvement of one's life and the lives
that one may touch be the most that
can be done?

What is in one's head has much to do
with what is in one's heart.

For Today and Tomorrow

*W*hat the human world is in most need of today is what it has always needed most: wisdom and love.

*O*nly on the day when no opportunity is passed by to add to the positives of life has one lived wholly in that day of one's life.

For Today and Tomorrow

All great virtues and ideals are the progeny of selflessness.

To give of oneself is not only to give what one has, but what one is in mind, heart and spirit.

For Today and Tomorrow

*T*o get to all there is inside you
you must give all there is of you to the
endeavor.

*H*ow deeply one has to reach into
oneself to reach the way of the eternal.

For Today and Tomorrow

*T*he structure of a life is built a day at a time, but only the eternal holds the foundation that can be sustained and built upon.

*O*ne cannot fritter away the days of one's life engaged with the trivial and be anywhere close to connection with the spiritual.

For Today and Tomorrow

*T*he allure of the temporal can be
strong, but for the enlightened spirit it has
no power, the allure of the spiritual
being so much stronger.

*T*here is no age to the spirit whose
focus is the exploration and expression
of the timeless.

For Today and Tomorrow

The depths of life you are willing to experience will always be up to you.

$y$ou are not only your music, but also the instrument of your music.

For Today and Tomorrow

*T*here is always another note to play
on the path of the spiritual.

*P*leasures can be found in the temporal;
bliss is the gift of the eternal.

For Today and Tomorrow

$\mathcal{T}$he day arrives for all to make of it
what they will.

$\mathcal{N}$ever will the possibilities for a day's
discoveries and creations of the profound
be exhausted.

For Today and Tomorrow

*I*s not the imperishable of life something to be revered and lived for . . .

*T*o live near the light is to find one's way through the darkness.

For Today and Tomorrow

The life lived through the spiritual is not free of difficulty, but never is it absent of gratitude.

To be grateful every moment for the true blessings of life is among the greatest of blessings.

For Today and Tomorrow

$\mathcal{T}$o just want to make it through the days is to just want to make it through life . . . does not the day (and life) deserve better?

$\mathcal{D}$ay-to-day living is day-to-day dying.

For Today and Tomorrow

A pearl of the spiritual is not seen by
the eye whose focus is on the temporal,
but it is not the pearl that is hiding.

The wise look to the harvest that is
found in all seasons.

For Today and Tomorrow

Non-response to much of the temporal is a response of wisdom.

To not let go of the perishable is to seal a fate of broken dreams.

For Today and Tomorrow

*T*o let go is to open, to release, to ease, to calm, to remove barriers barring the way to higher growth.

*W*hat room is there for growth or fulfillment in the life that is filled with the fleeting?

For Today and Tomorrow

True life runs counter to the artificiality that dominates everyday life.

When it is realized that the fleeting of the world is farce, façade, deception, an invitation to nowhere, it can no longer encroach upon living through the eternal of one's life.

For Today and Tomorrow

*T*he goings-on of the passing really do mean nothing; the realm of the eternal really does mean everything.

*T*o move one's life from the temporal to the eternal is like moving from arid land to a grand oasis.

For Today and Tomorrow

*T*hey never reach the promised land who take the journey through fear and not love.

*W*hat is imposed will not last; what is accepted blindly, will not last; what is done without sincerity, reverence, devotion, sacrifice, will not last.

For Today and Tomorrow

The seed doesn't grow from outside to inside, from above to below.

Where to go but to yourself to find your true wealth and tend to the spiritual of your life?

For Today and Tomorrow

$\mathcal{T}$o escape the false of the world one must turn inward, but not to hide — to confront, to grow, to create, to harvest; to discover the deepest truths by way of the spiritual journey . . . (the inner journey).

$\mathcal{W}$hat rises from inner depths can rival all from the world that is of the surface.

For Today and Tomorrow

*M*any never get to the depths of themselves because they never take the time or make the effort to create them.

*T*he true casualties of life are not the lives that are cut short or struck by great affliction, but those that are lived from beginning to end not knowing their true power, realized by taking the journey within.

For Today and Tomorrow

*T*o have never journeyed into oneself is to have travelled all of one's days in the wrong direction.

*B*efore knowing the answers to one's life one must know what the questions are, and they can only be found within.

For Today and Tomorrow

The stakes are always high in the spiritual.

They cannot lay claim to the keys to life's best who stake their lives in the temporal.

For Today and Tomorrow

With every want of the fleeting
relinquished, life's possibilities increase.

To be obsessed with the trivial
is for a human being like an animal
foraging in the dirt, an inch at a time.

For Today and Tomorrow

*T*o refuse to let go of the petty is to never know the profound.

A person is the measure of his or her depth (or lack thereof).

For Today and Tomorrow

*T*he wise let nothing keep them from the inner work that will lead them to the best of themselves, for they know that anything they do before this has earnestly begun cannot be of true value to themselves or anyone else.

*E*ither realized or waiting to be realized, there is a life within all that is larger than all that fades before them.

For Today and Tomorrow

*H*ollow is the essence of the material.

*W*hat is forever is also forever new.

For Today and Tomorrow

It is illusion that rules the day in the life that is lived through the temporal.

One can be most active in the day-to-day of life and yet be spiritually asleep.

For Today and Tomorrow

$\mathcal{D}$ay-to-day life takes so much more than it gives to human life.

$\mathcal{T}$hey get it who realize that it is not about getting from the temporal, but serving the eternal.

For Today and Tomorrow

The best of what can be of you does not belong to only you.

To be free of attachments to the temporal is not to be free of caring for those who make it their home.

For Today and Tomorrow

*D*oes not the best of human life depend on discovering one's best, and helping others along the way to do the same?

*Y*ou did not give yourself life, it is something that was given to you . . . should not the giving continue to be passed on, giving the energies of your life to the service of something that you are a part of, yet is greater than yourself?

For Today and Tomorrow

*T*he discovery of love, truth, wisdom and
beauty of a spiritual nature isn't enough —
it must also be lived and ever explored.

*T*o place your life in the service of the
eternal is to live that part of you untouched
by time and death.

For Today and Tomorrow

*I*t matters not what day it is when the eternal is the guiding presence of one's life.

*T*hey have no fear of death who live close to the heart and spirit.

For Today and Tomorrow

*T*he spiritually evolved ask nothing of life
but the opportunity to continue to grow so
they may continue to give.

*E*ach day (each moment) arrives with
the gift of life's creative force — are you
partaking of the gift . . .

For Today and Tomorrow

The promise of something better is not somewhere other, it is here, now, to be made better within and without.

He is not rich who doesn't know what to do with his wealth.

For Today and Tomorrow

The higher the wisdom the more it is governed by the heart.

One who has lived in darkness may leave the world on the brightest of days, but still leaves his life in a state of darkness.

*O*f the face of evil it is greed that takes up the greater part.

*K*indness is the smile of the soul.

For Today and Tomorrow

*K*indness is a gift that anyone at any time can give to another.

*I*f you are dissatisfied with facets of life or the world, what are you doing today and every day to lessen the measure of what dissatisfies you?

For Today and Tomorrow

*F*or everything one cannot do for the betterment of life there is something one can do.

*C*ompassion is always beautiful.

For Today and Tomorrow

*I*t costs so little to be benevolent toward others, yet so much damage is done to the world because of a daily dearth of benevolence.

*I*f one knew nothing else, did nothing else but to give of oneself in the spirit of selflessness, one would live a life of grace as few can be lived.

For Today and Tomorrow

What a great thing the good heart is.

True life [spiritual life] is always ready to receive and be received.

For Today and Tomorrow

What changes a life profoundly is
becoming aware of, then connecting to
the unchanging of the eternal.

Ego is the barrier that keeps the eyes
from seeing, the heart from feeling, the
mind from comprehending the majesty
of Life.

For Today and Tomorrow

*W*hen ego is done away with, the best
of human-being begins its realization.

*T*he preparedness to grow is only the
beginning . . . it must be accompanied by
a willingness to engage in inner work,
led to the chore by humility for growth
to be achieved.

For Today and Tomorrow

What difference would it make to
live in a mansion if one's inner house
were as a dilapidated building lying in
ruins from neglect?

The loss to their lives is immeasurable
who fail to care for the spiritual dimension
of their lives.

For Today and Tomorrow

*I*f one were in need of rice a thousand
fields of wheat would not fulfill the need.
And so it is with the spiritual needs of a life,
unable to be fulfilled by anything not of
the spiritual.

*E*ach day is a call to Life — a challenge
to serve with devotion the true, the profound,
the eternal.

For Today and Tomorrow

*W*hy seek the mastering of the fleeting when serving the eternal rises above all glories of the here today, gone tomorrow?

*S*ervants of the eternal know a grace of heart and spirit unknown to the power-seeker of the temporal.

For Today and Tomorrow

When appearance is all-important to opening a door, what is behind it will likely be little more than appearance.

Nothing of the eternal wants to buy or sell you — this, the interest of the temporal.

For Today and Tomorrow

*E*arthly ambitions . . . are they not all tied too closely to the animality of human–being to be the way to go?

*W*hat one takes seriously demonstrates how serious one is in matters of spiritual growth.

For Today and Tomorrow

The spiritual shuts no one out, keeps
no one at bay. One prevents or allows
oneself passage to it and to what degree,
by what one does and doesn't do throughout
his or her days.

The commitment to Life covers all
essential commitments.

For Today and Tomorrow

*T*he enlightened have always focused on what of yesterday that remains today and will still be tomorrow, not the banalities from the carnival of the day-to-day that soon pass into oblivion.

*A*ll must decide for themselves if they are to live only as temporal beings, or as living manifests of the eternal.

For Today and Tomorrow

One is either part of the flame of Existence, or part of its smoke.

How can one be true, be whole until the false of the world has been banished from one's life?

For Today and Tomorrow

*H*igher awareness comes from the depths of inner being.

*O*ne cannot see the false from the true until the inner light has been reached.

For Today and Tomorrow

You do not have to go anywhere but where you are to find your way to the eternal of your life, for it is always with you, inside you, waiting for your discovery.

More rewarding than the awareness attained from the inner journey is the spirituality that continues to grow and bless.

For Today and Tomorrow

*T*hey never draw near to the infinite who are more interested in the real estate that they can stand on than the estate of their mind and spirit.

*T*o take one's work for one's life is healthy if of a spiritual nature, unhealthy if it is not.

For Today and Tomorrow

*L*ife doesn't rush, doesn't stall, doesn't wait — it moves on steadily, accommodating all at an even pace, being up to all to do with the time that they are given.

*E*very day draws one closer to the end of one's days . . . should not the most of it be made?

For Today and Tomorrow

*C*rops from the temporal of a life are poor as well as fleeting.

*F*or those whose lives are lived through the eternal, today is part of yesterday and tomorrow.

For Today and Tomorrow

*T*o relate with only the temporal
of another is to make no connection of
significance to the other.

*I*s it not both odd and futile to build
an entire life on what will one day be
no more?

For Today and Tomorrow

$\mathcal{T}$o choose the fleeting over the eternal is to turn the story of one's life into the fleeting.

$\mathcal{T}$he life lived through all its power approaches its sunset with its dawn still burning in its heart.

For Today and Tomorrow

*O*f the temporal all things come to pass, including the human form, but the human spirit has the power to create and unite with what will not pass away.

*P*ower, yes — the impetus of life . . . spiritual power, creative power, drawing from the soul of selflessness.

For Today and Tomorrow

*T*o live to the fullest is to live one's days to the deepest.

*I*t is not in one's command to assign a value to one's life, but it is to create it.

For Today and Tomorrow

How much spiritual wealth is forfeited daily throughout humankind for a pseudo-wealth of the ephemeral.

Where everything else pales in comparison . . . is this not where humankind needs to be?

For Today and Tomorrow

One need not be a prophet or a saint to live for truth, for love, for beauty, for Life.

The condition for entry into the spiritual is sincerity in wanting to grow.

For Today and Tomorrow

The day may be lived with good thoughts or evil thoughts, kind gestures or mean gestures, base deeds or noble deeds.

The greater the spirit the greater the humility.

For Today and Tomorrow

When there is love in one's soul what day is not worth living? Is not worth serving?

Humility is at every point, at every change that elevates human life.

For Today and Tomorrow

*J*ust one beautiful day is worth the pains of life if one has the depth of mind and spirit to behold its magnificence.

*T*here is sorrow in genuine love, but no darkness, only light yearning to project as far as it can go.

For Today and Tomorrow

*I*f you pray, pray not to be protected
from pain, from strife, from tribulation,
but from hindrance to the best of you,
and the prayer that is Life.

*T*he only path for a human being that
matters is the one that leads to the death
of the ego and the way of the spiritual.

For Today and Tomorrow

*T*he journey creates the strength that is needed to continue on the journey.

*B*eyond measure is the distance of value from the offerings of the temporal to those of the eternal.

For Today and Tomorrow

The greatest treasures do not come to one,
one must go to them — in the heights . . . in
the depths.

When the journey is of a profound nature
even the deepest sorrows are of paradise.

For Today and Tomorrow

A life most blessed is one that is able to give all it has to give, express all it has to express.

Accept the pains of growth and watch the riches flow.

For Today and Tomorrow

*I*f you persevere, meeting your days
with love and courage, know that Life
will not fail to be with you.

*W*ill you live to the end through the
light of the never ending . . .

For Today and Tomorrow

*D*oing what you can for the World . . .
waking every day to the life that is yours,
to the world that is you.

ABOUT THE AUTHOR

Carroll Blair is an author of more than twenty
books and the recipient of numerous awards.
His work has been well endorsed and com-
mendably reviewed. Among his titles cited
for distinction are *Through the Shadows*, winner
of the Pacific Book Awards, and *Quarter Notes*,
winner of the Sharp Writ Book Awards.
He is an alumnus of the Boston Conservatory
and lives in Massachusetts.